Book of Word and Picture Puzzles

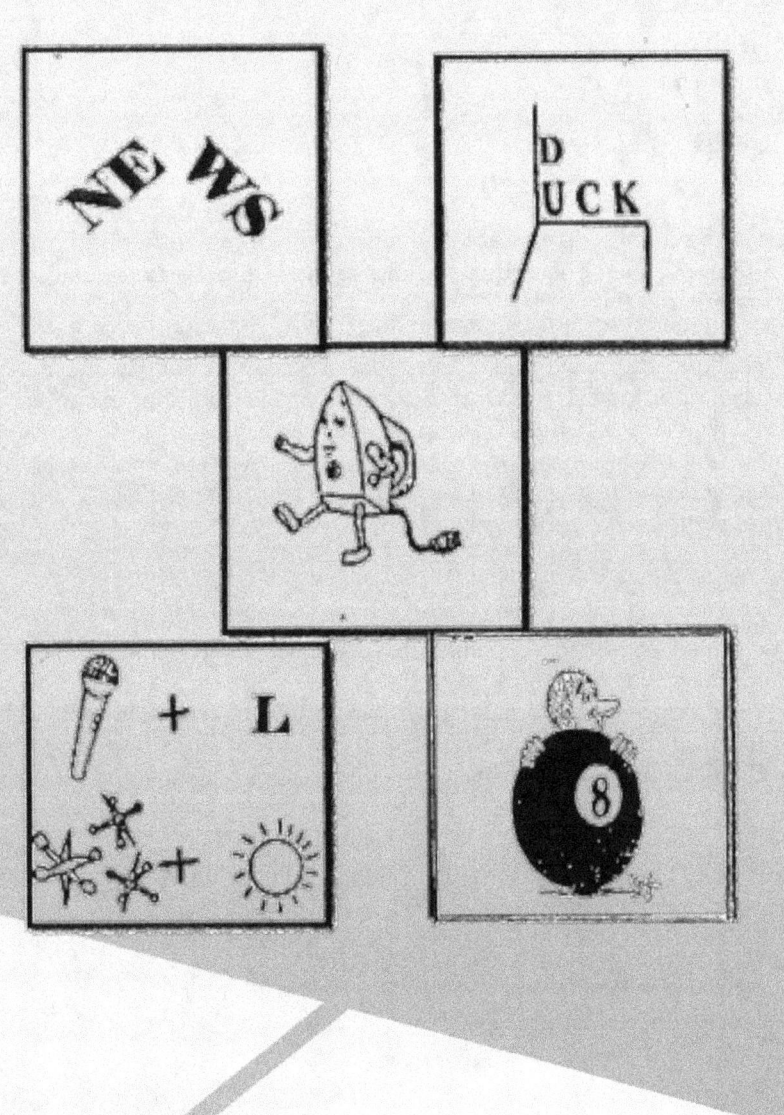

Book of Word and Picture Puzzles
All Rights Reserved.
Copyright © 2020 O. B. Parker
v1.0

The opinions expressed in this manuscript are solely the opinions of the author and do not represent the opinions or thoughts of the publisher. The author has represented and warranted full ownership and/or legal right to publish all the materials in this book.

This book may not be reproduced, transmitted, or stored in whole or in part by any means, including graphic, electronic, or mechanical without the express written consent of the publisher except in the case of brief quotations embodied in critical articles and reviews.

Outskirts Press, Inc.
http://www.outskirtspress.com

ISBN: 978-1-9772-1886-5

Cover Photo © 2020 O. B. Parker. All Rights Reserved – Used With Permission.

Outskirts Press and the "OP" logo are trademarks belonging to Outskirts Press, Inc.

PRINTED IN THE UNITED STATES OF AMERICA

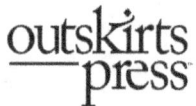

Introduction

The word and picture puzzles in this book are intended to help develop critical thinking skills and pose a fun challenge for kids and adults. They are designed to be an exciting instructional tool for classrooms that includes a variety of different types of learners and for adults and kids to explore thought outside the logical thinking box.

Test your skills and those of others in stimulating the mind to discover new and old euphemistic expressions along with media and musical history. You will be able to learn and have fun at the same time.

Enjoy these quick fun activities. You can even use them as icebreakers or create your own game show. Work together as a team and share information as you attempt to solve the puzzles. It's always fun to see the answers and be amazed at how close you came to solving them.

At the same time, you will develop skills to help you look at things in a different perspective and with a new understanding.

Dedicated to:

    Raymond, Jeff, Big Free and David

Thanks guys for the inspiration, the unknowing input and all those crazy times which tied this all together.

Acknowledge

Would like to acknowledge the contributions made by
Dr. Ramona Mebane and Mr. Gary Doyle.

CONTENTS

Word and Figure Expressions... Pages 5-8

Word and Picture Expressions ....Pages 9-11

Picture Puzzle Expressions.. Pages 12--14

Sports Expressions... Page 15

Personalities ....Page 16

Song Title Expressions...Pages 17-18

TV Show Expressions.. Pages 19-20

Movie Expressions.. Pages 21-22

Potpourri ....Pages 23-24

Puzzle Answers..Page 25

Puzzles Description

The puzzles in this book are objects that you must decipher the hidden meaning of each set of words/ pictures found in each box. They can include movie or TV titles and all sorts of famous expressions and antidotes. Pay attention to the scripted categories and keep that in mind when attempting to solve each puzzle.

Word and Figure Expressions

Decipher the hidden meaning of each set of words/pictures

1 STONE	2 new ᖴ∀ƎꞀ (LEAF upside down)	3 (LAST in circle) ↑	4 SLEEP (wavy)
5 NE WS (tilted)	6 TE∆SE	7 GOD / 1 USA ; 3⃠5	8 1999 2000
9 ⚭ PEOPLE→ same ←PEOPLE	10 EV EN (tilted)	11 Hairline	12 (T H R T U in circle)
13 E N E M I E E S (scattered)	14 MURNING (upside down)	15 JOKE (vertical)	16 getting ↑ da ʜn

Word and Figure Expressions

Decipher the hidden meaning of each set of words/pictures

1 **Past** (with "a" blurred/overlapping)	2 safety (with numbers 1-9 scattered around in a circle)	3 G o s p e l	4 ROGER OUT OVER
5 365 check ↑	6 BATHING SUIT	7 the market	8 head in love heels
9 D ngue U C K (on chair)	10 to ngue ngue	11 (circle) drinks house	12 meal snack meal
13 (panic in circle)	14 Aluminum (vertical)	15 Ac+ (Ac with t, c lower)	16 (Applause in circle)

8

Word and Figure Expressions

Decipher the hidden meaning of each set of words/pictures

1. 3 + 2 = risk	2. ESCAPE (vertical)	3. E(O)GO	4. WHAT ↑↓
5. It's ⊘ CRACKED↑ 2 be	6. ⬛ IN	7. B ⊘ GOOD	8. ⊘ ands buts ifs
9. Willow ¦ ¦	10. times behind	11. hold / second	12. animation
13. ↻	14. sugar / pretty please	15. OVATION (vertical)	16. arrest you're

Word and Figure Expressions

Decipher the hidden meaning of each set of words/pictures

1 (5¢) & (10¢) ....ing	2 eyebrows	3 GET A WORD IN (vertical)	4 Block
5 School	6 = RIGHTS	7 Eggs easy	8 DRY
9 Amen	10 jinks	11 sec ond timing	12 ⊘ ? asked
13 G o s s i p	14 SKPIEY	15 ⊘ Return	16 MIRROR (vertical)

Words and Pictures Expressions

Decipher the hidden meaning of each set of words/pictures

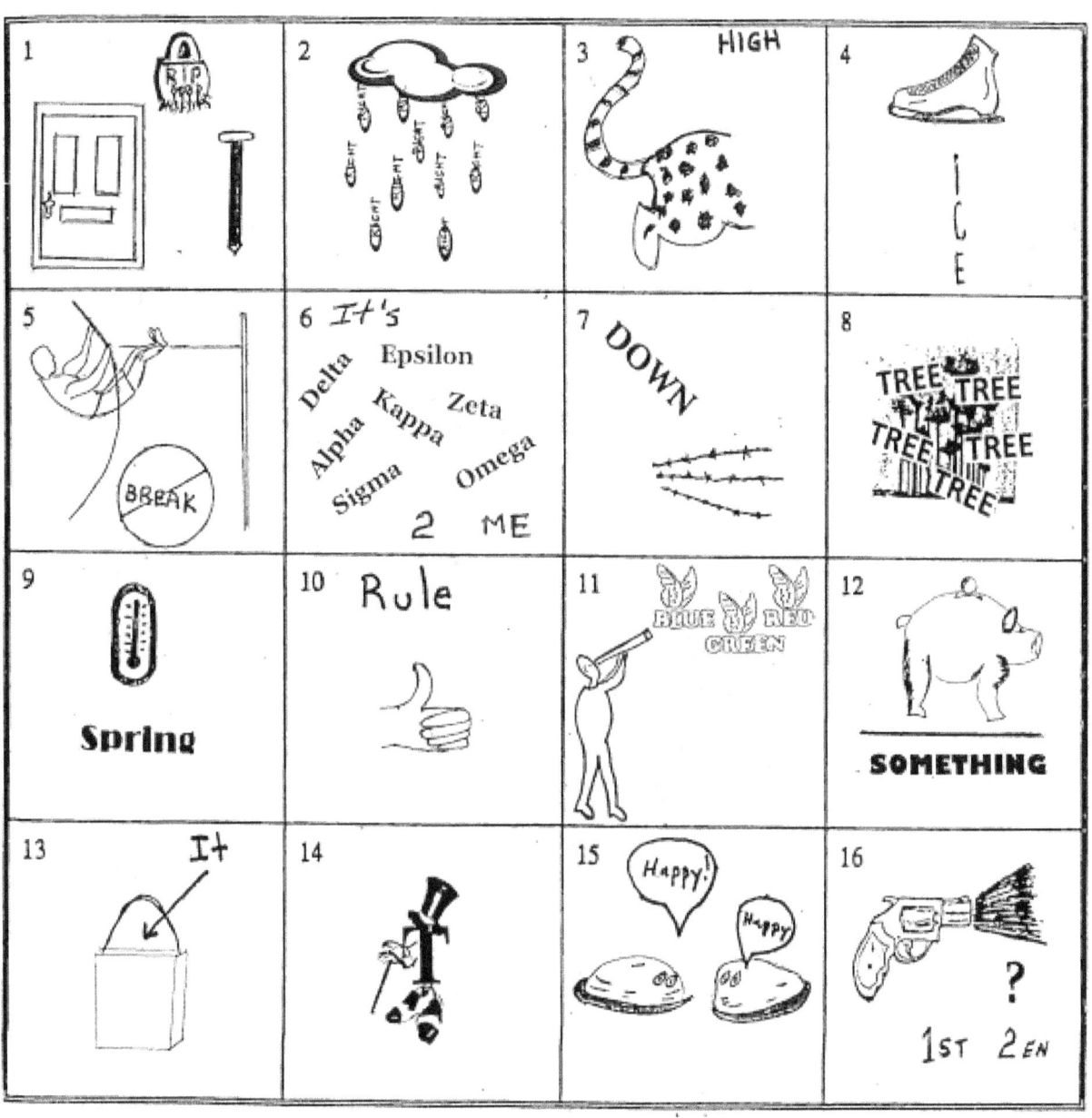

Words and Pictures Expressions

Decipher the hidden meaning of each set of words/pictures

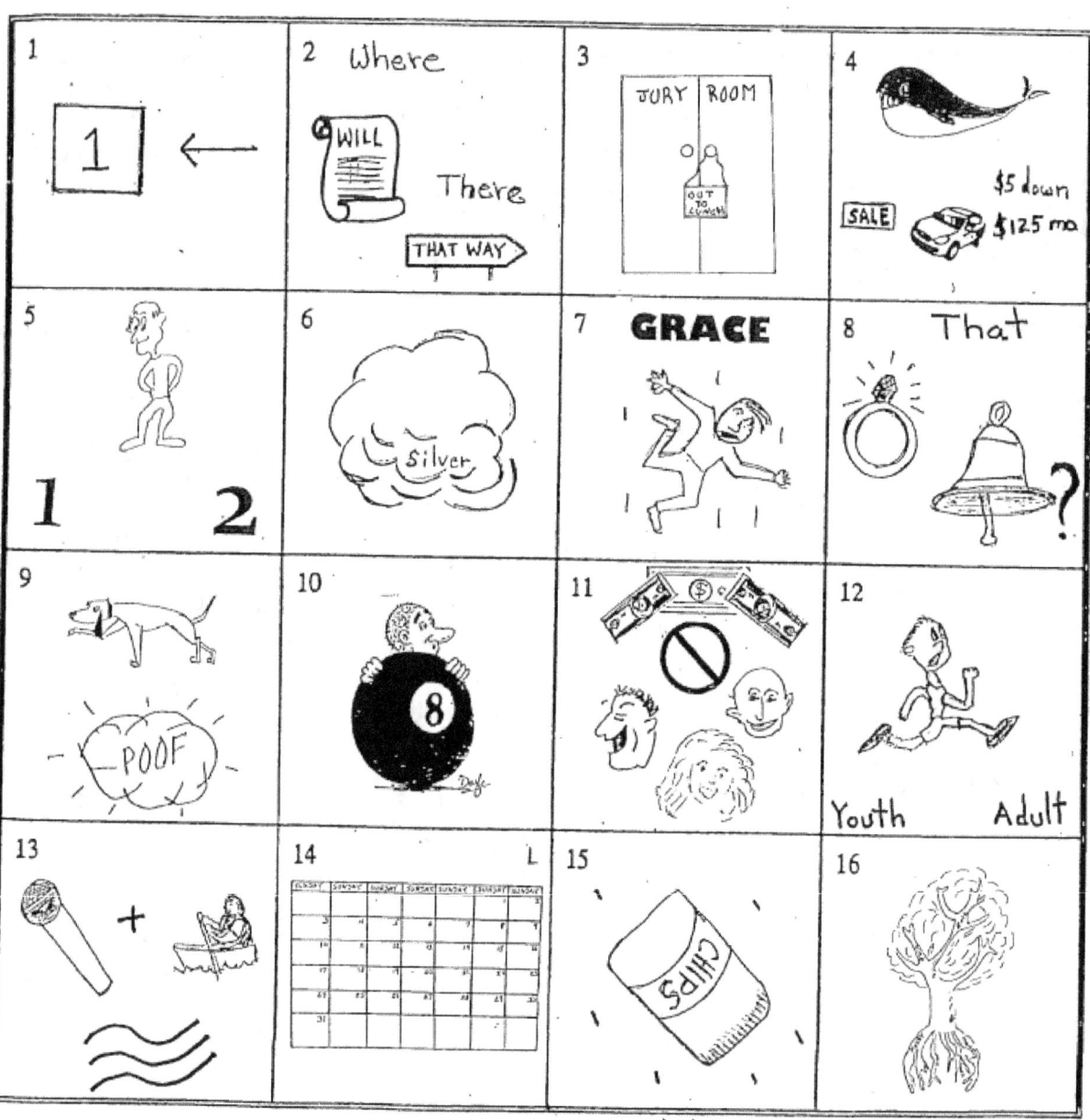

Words and Pictures Expressions

Decipher the hidden meaning of each set of words/pictures

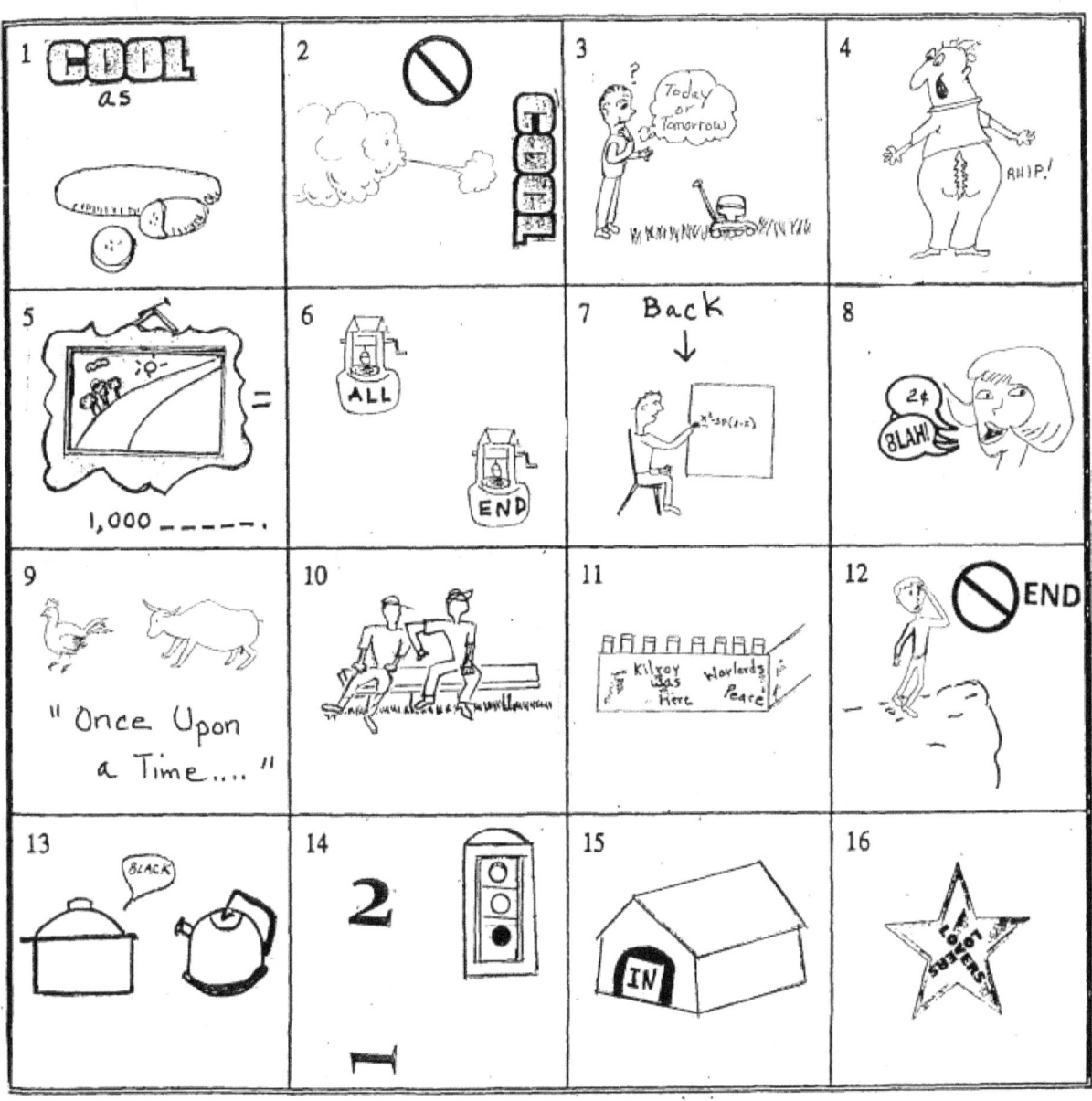

Pictures Puzzle Expressions

Decipher the hidden meaning of each set of words/pictures. whey can include movie and TV titles.

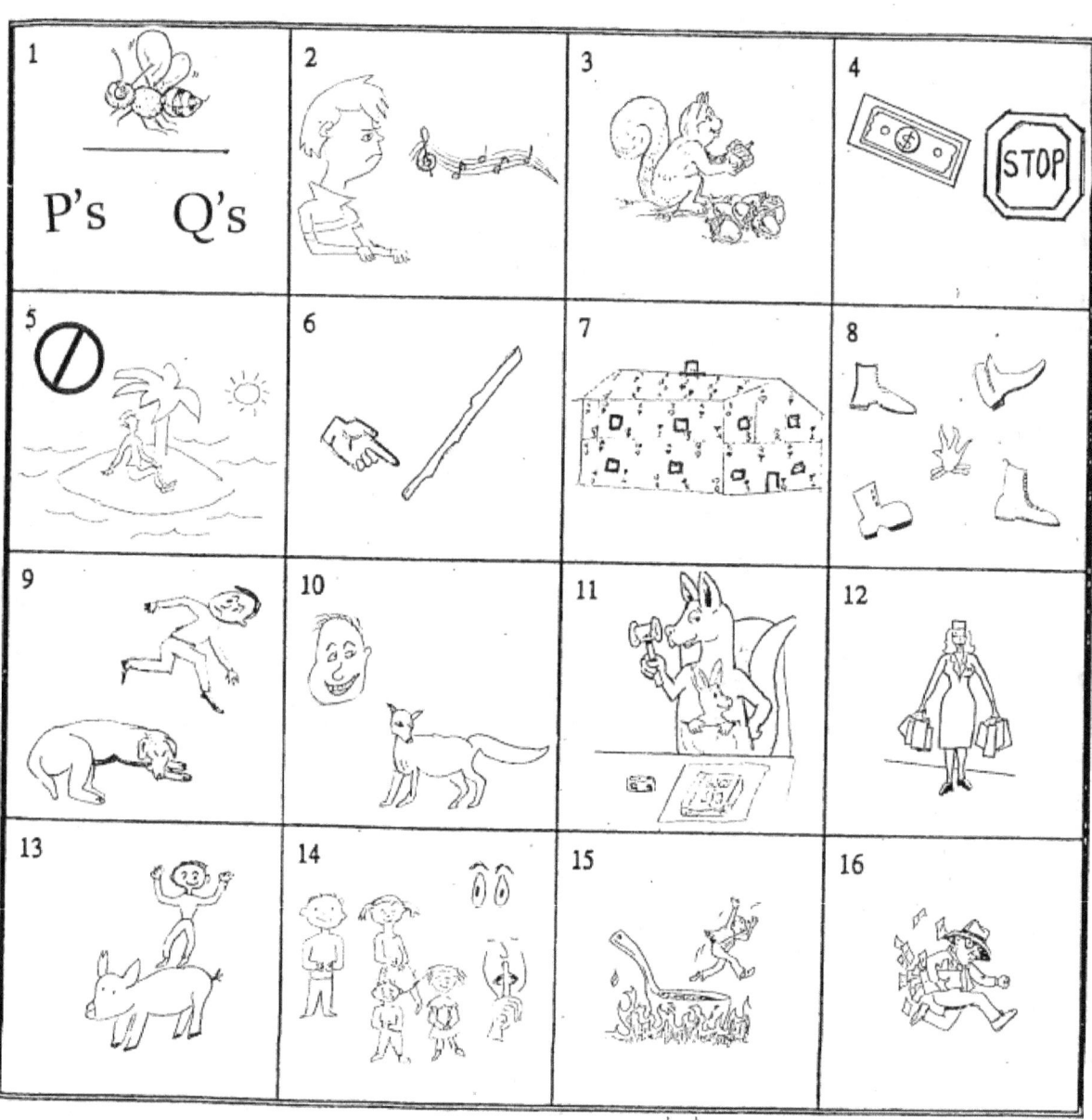

Pictures Puzzle Expressions

Decipher the hidden meaning of each set of words/pictures. whey can include movie and TV titles.

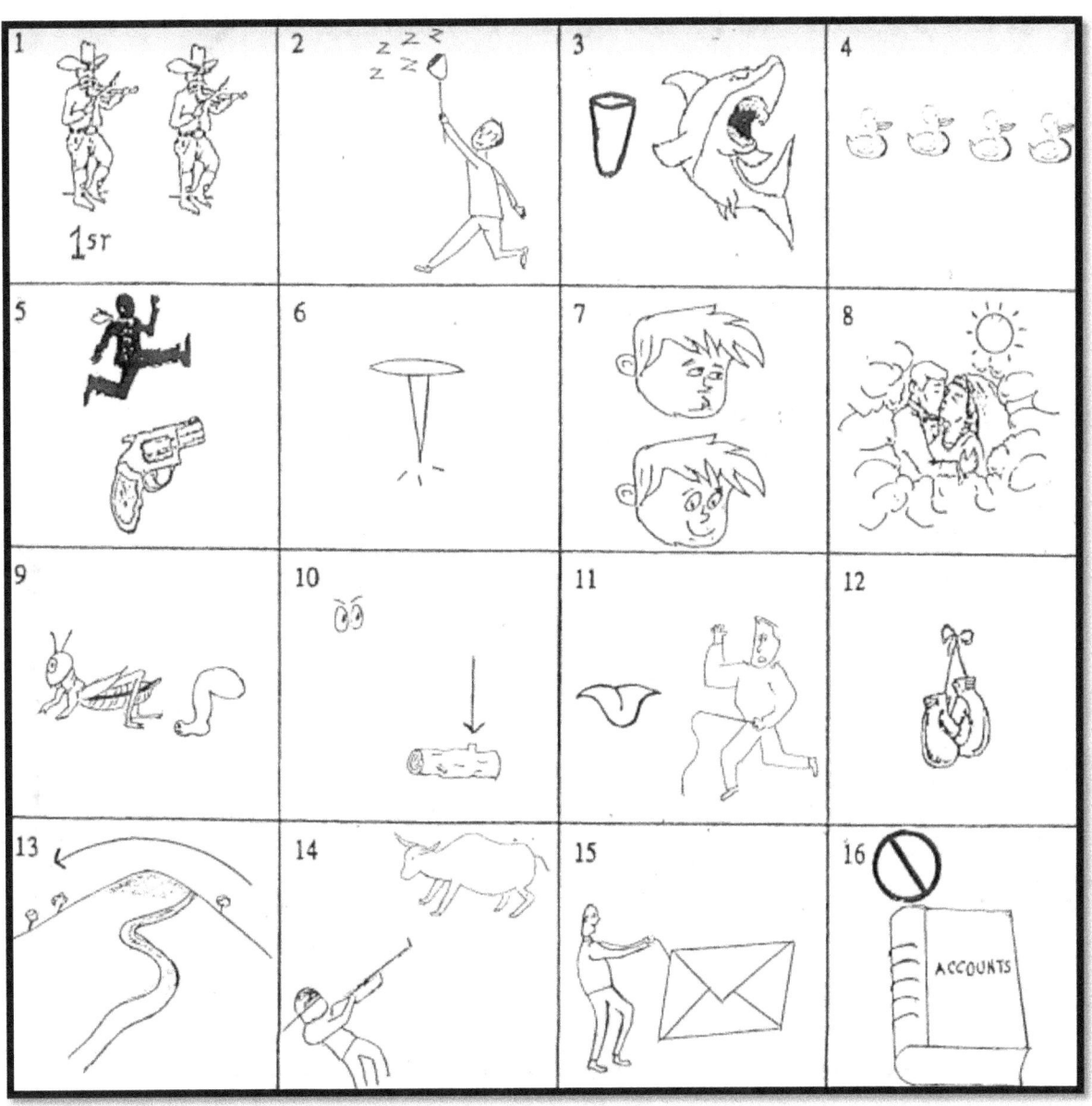

Pictures Puzzle Expressions

Decipher the hidden meaning of each set of words/pictures. whey can include movie and TV titles.

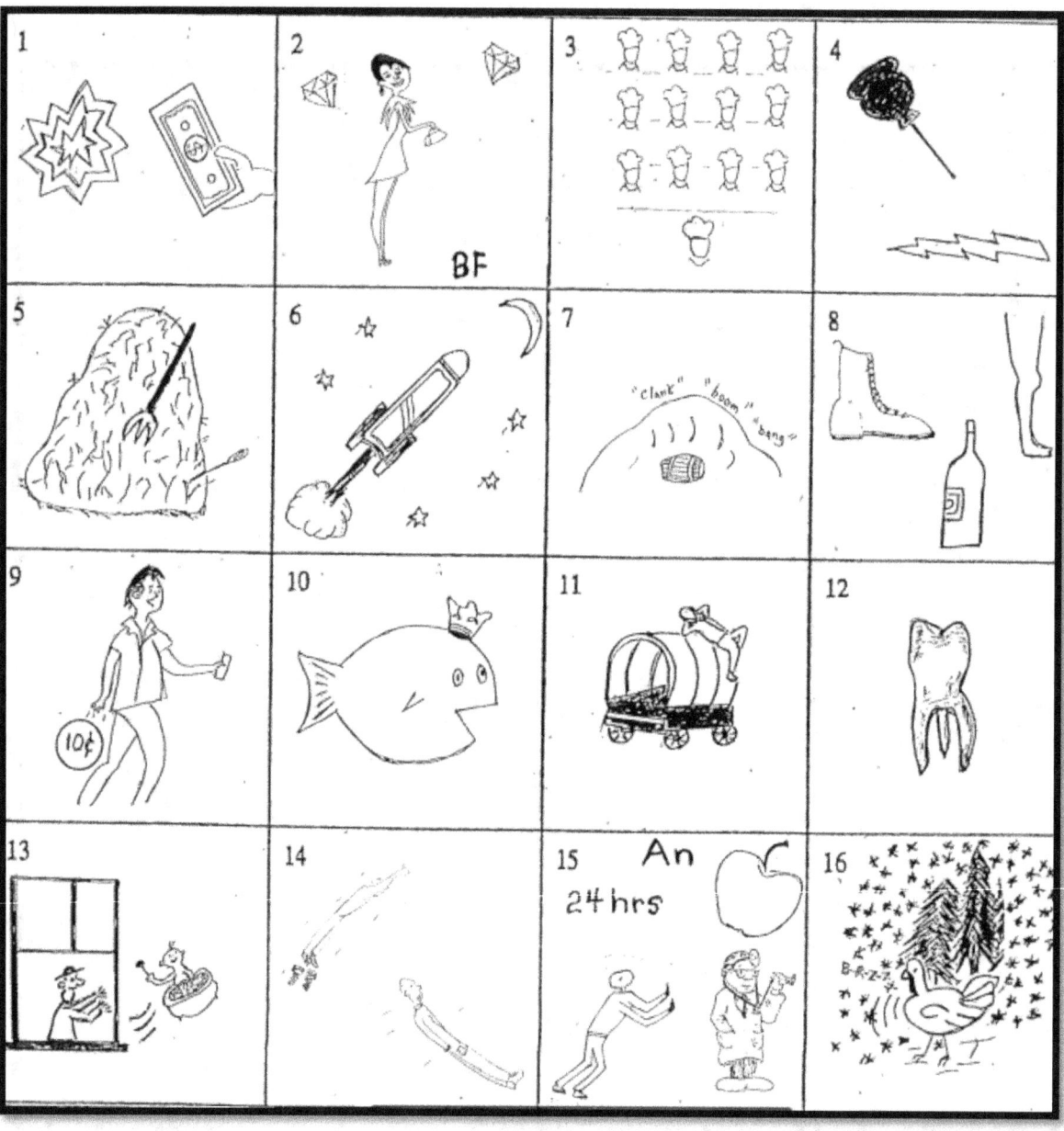

Sport Expressions

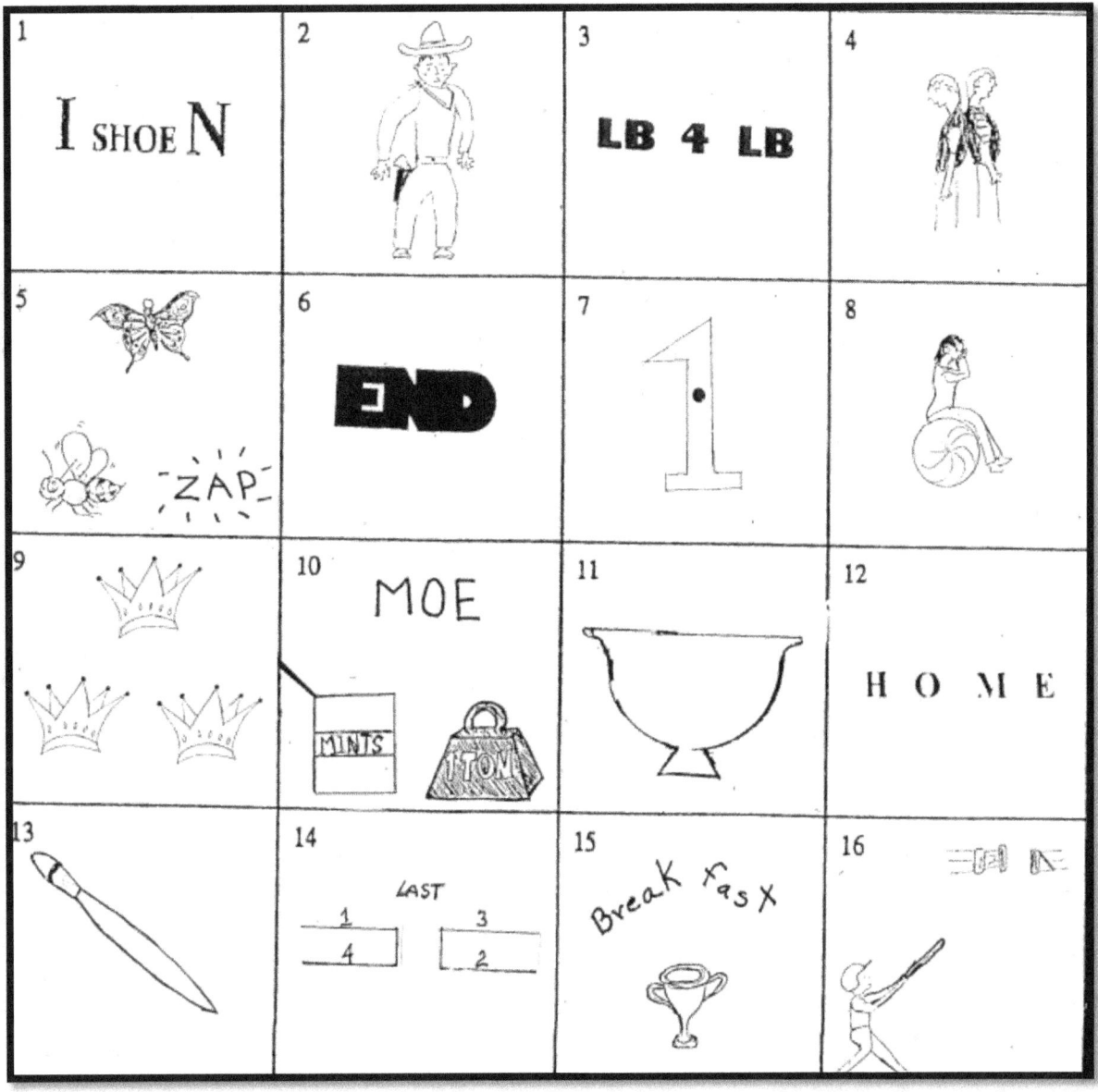

PERSONALITIES

18

SONG TITLE EXPRESSIONS

SONG TITLE EXPRESSIONS

20

TV Show Expressions

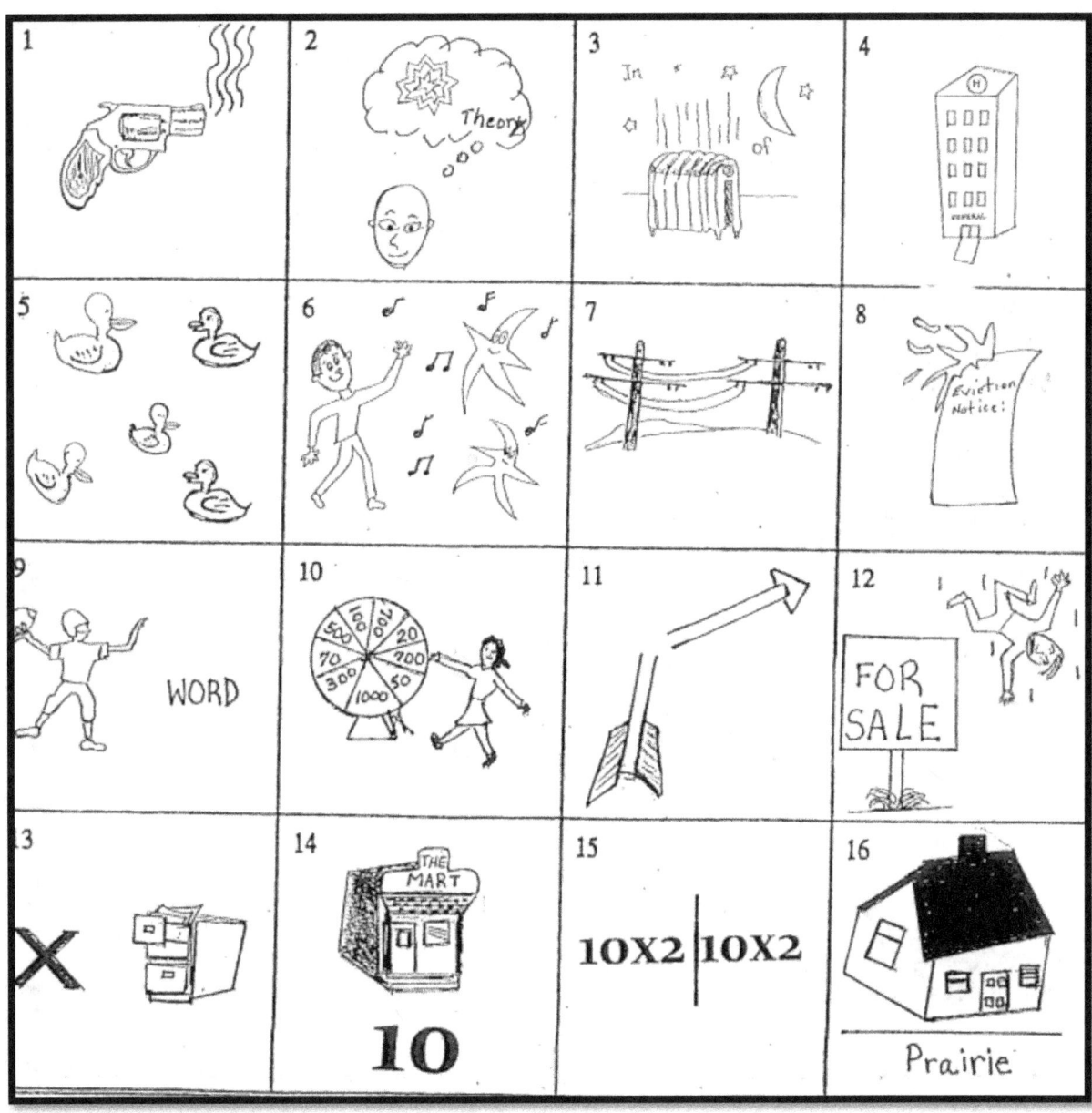

TV Show Expressions

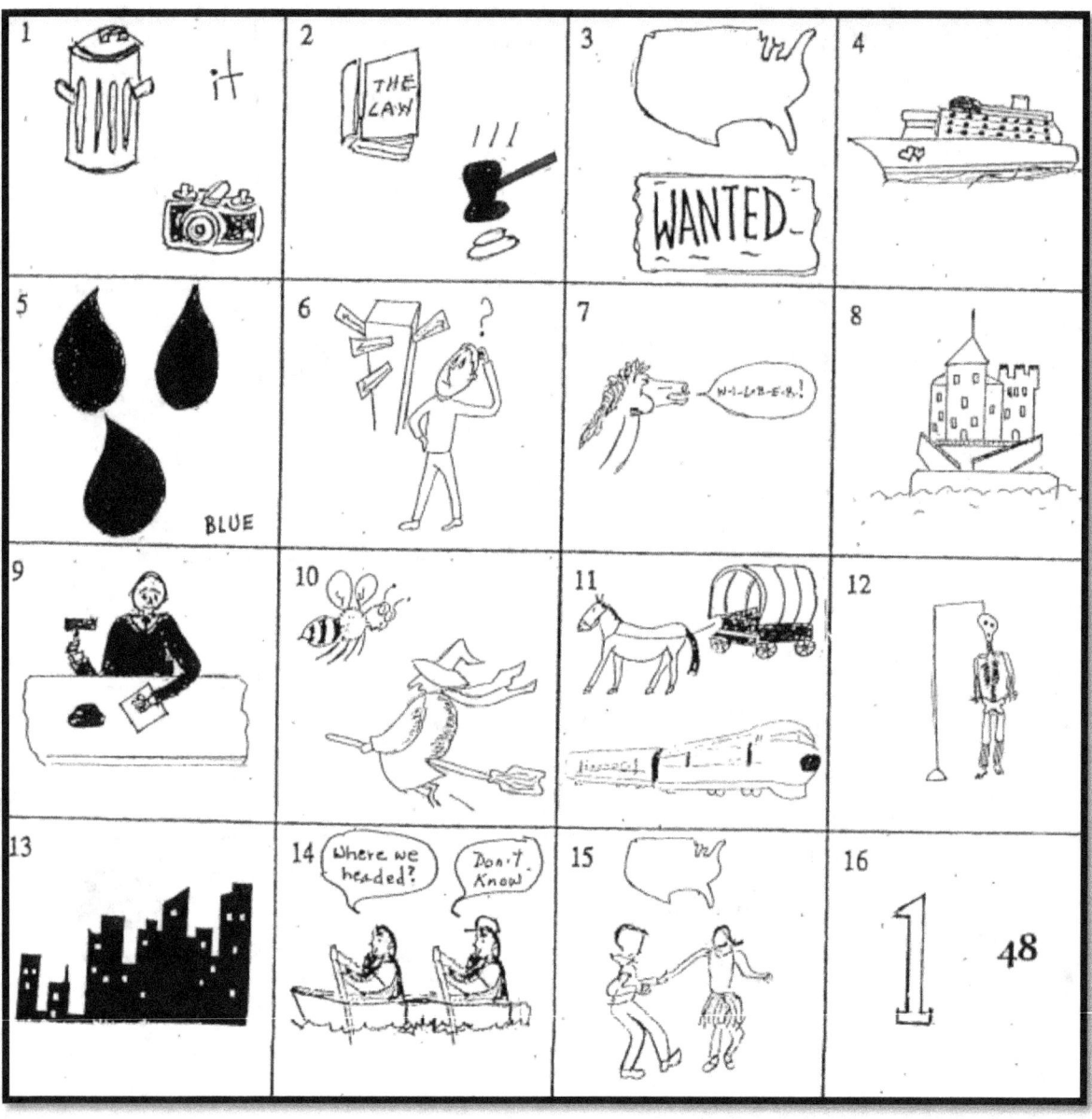

Movie Expressions

1	2	3	4 FUTURE ←
5	6 PURPLE	7 (PETER)	8
9 (DESIRE)	10	11	12 The ..... Hundred
13	14 POOF!	15	16 "wanna go HOME"

MOVIE EXPRESSIONS

Potpourri

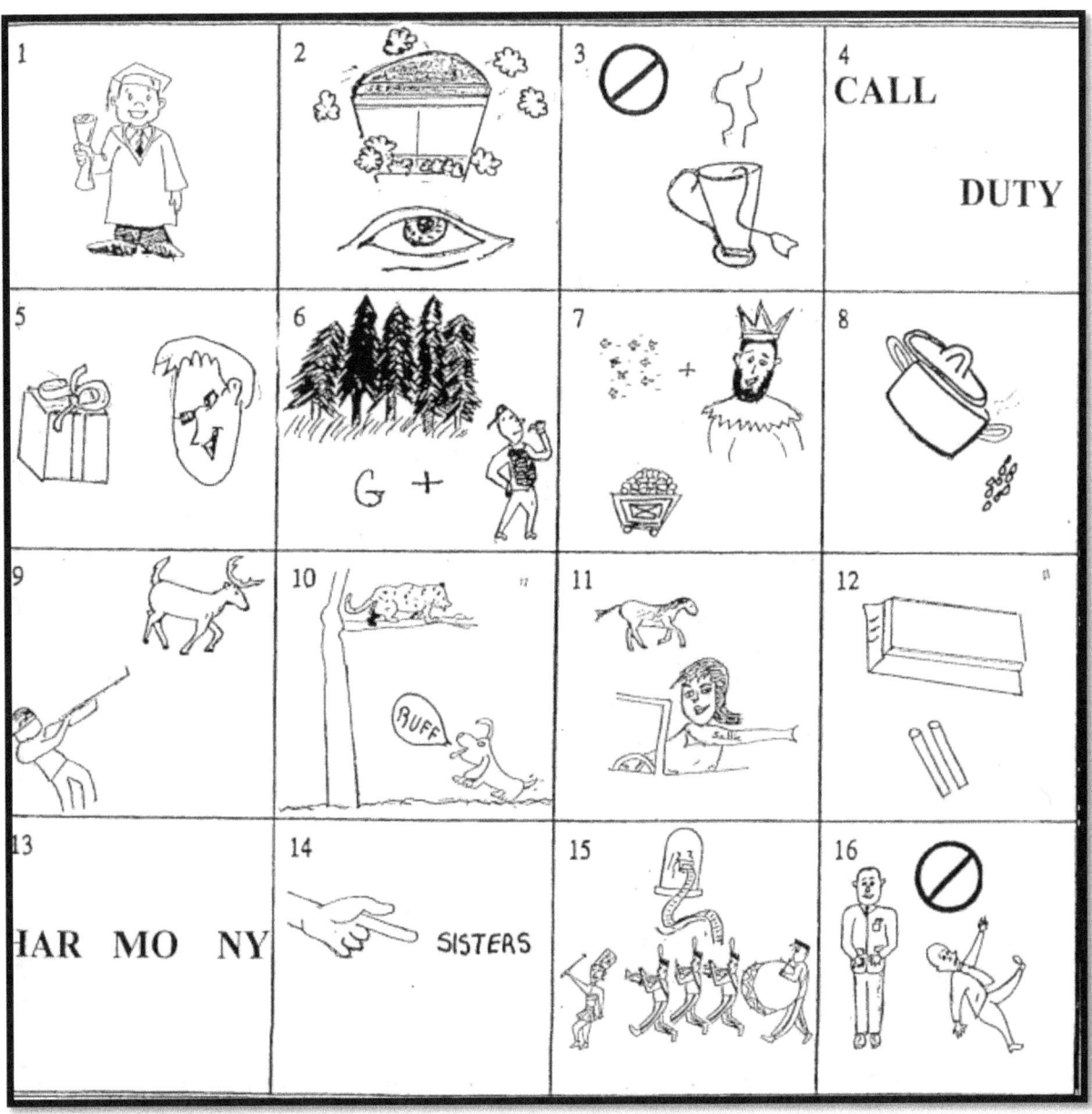

POTPOURRI

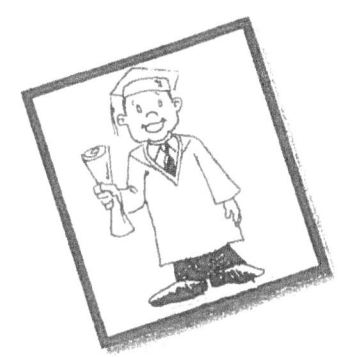
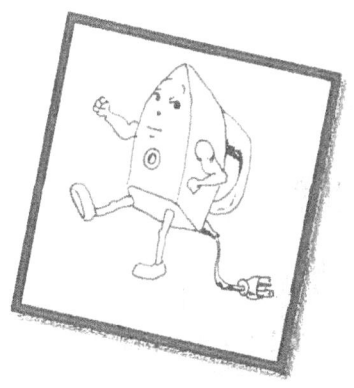

Answers to the Puzzles

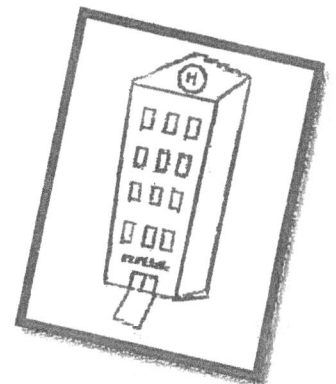
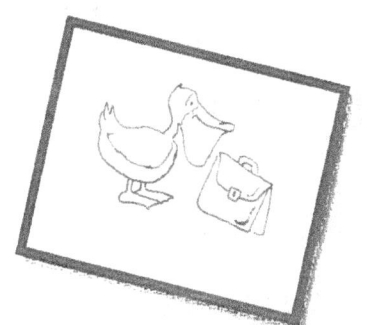

Word and Figure Expressions

Page 1

1. Cornerstone
2. Turning over a new leaf
3. The last roundup
4. Sleep tight
5. Breaking news
6. Striptease
7. One nation under God indivisible
8. Turn of the century
9. See the same people on the way up that you see on the way down
10. Breaking even
11. Receding hairline
12. Circle of truth
13. Arch enemies
14. Top of the morning
15. Side splitting joke
16. Getting up at the crack of dawn

Word and Figure Expressions
Page 2

1. Checkered past
2. Safety in numbers
3. Spreading the gospel
4. Roger, over and out
5. Yearly checkup
6. Topless bathing suit
7. Corner market
8. Head over heels in love
9. Sitting duck
10. Forked tongue
11. A round of drinks on the house
12. In between meal snack
13. Panic button
14. Aluminum siding
15. Disappearing act
16. A round of applause

Word and Figure Expressions
Page 3

1. Calculated risk

2. Narrow escape

3. Inflated ego

4. What goes up must come down

5. It's not what it is cracked up to be

6. In the black

7. To be up to no good

8. No ifs, ands or buts

9. Weeping willow

10. Behind the times

11. Hold on a second

12. Suspended animation

13. Counter clockwise

14. Pretty please with sugar on top

15. Standing ovation

16. You're under arrest

Words and Pictures
Page 4

1. Nickel and diming

2. Raise eyebrows

3. Get a word in edgewise

4. Chip off the old block

5. High school

6. Equal rights

7. Eggs over easy

8. High and dry

9. Amen corner

10. High jinks

11. Split-second timing

12. No questions asked

13. Gossip column

14. Pie in sky

15. Point of no return

16. Full length mirror

Words and Pictures
Page 5

1. Dead as a door nail

2. Right as rain

3. High tailing it

4. Skating on thin ice

5. Bend but don't break

6. It's Greek to me

7. Down to the wire

8. Can't see the forest for the trees

9. Spring break

10, Rule of thumb

11.Seeing flying colors

12. Bank on something

13. It's in the bag

14. Dressed to a T

15. Happy as a clam

16. Shoot first, ask questions later

Words and Picture Expressions
Page 6

1. Back to squares

2. Where there's a will, there's a way

3. The jury is out

4. A whale of a deal

5. The old 1,2

6. A cloud with a silver lining

7. Fall from grace

8. That, ring a bell?

9. Doggone

10. Behind the eight ball

11. Money can't buy happiness

12. Don't rush to get old

13. Microwave

14. A month of Sundays

15. The chips are down

16. Money is the root of all evil

Word and Picture Expressions
Page 7

1. Cool as a cucumber

2. Don't blow your cool

3. Don't put off until tomorrow, what you can do today

4. Too big for his britches

5. A picture is worth a 1000 words

6. All's well that ends well

7. Back to the drawing board

8. Putting her two cents worth in

9. Cock and bull story

10. The bench/benchwarmers

11. Writing on the wall

12. No end in sight

13. Pot calling the kettle black

14. One down, two to go

15. In the dog house

16. Star crossed lovers

Picture Puzzle Expressions
Page 8

1. Be on your P's and Q's

2. Face the music

3. Squirrel Nuts

4. The buck stops here

5. No man is an island

6. Short end of the stick

7. House of cards

8. Boot camp

9. Let sleeping dogs lie

10. Sly as a fox

11. Kangaroo court

12. Bag lady

13. High on the hog

14. Children should be seen not heard

15. Jumping from the frying pan into the fire

16. Take the money and run

Picture Puzzle Expressions
Page 9

1. Play second fiddle

2. Catching some z's

3. Glass jaw

4. Ducks In a row

5. Jumping the gun

6. Sharp as a tack

7. Don't be sad, be happy

8. Marriage made in heaven

9. Knee High to a Grasshopper

10. Looking like a Bump on a Log

11. Tongue Lashing

12. Hanging up the gloves

13. Over the hill

14. Shooting the bull

15. Pushing the envelope

16. No account

Picture Puzzle Expressions
Page 10

1. More bang for your buck

2. Diamonds are a girl's best friend

3. Baker's dozen

4. Greased lightening

5. A needle in a haystack

6. Shoot for the moon, If you don't make it you will be among the stars

7. Empty barrels make the most noise

S. Bootleg liquor

9. Dropping a dime

10. Kingfish

11. On the wagon

12. Long in the tooth

13. Throwing the baby out with the bath water

14. Spring forward, fall backwards

15. An apple a day keeps the doctor away

16. Cold turkey

Sports Expressions
Page 11

1. Shoo in

2. Gunslinger

3. Pound for pound

4. Back to back

5. Float like a butterfly, sting like a bee

6. Tight end

7. Hole-in-one

8. On the ball

9. The Triple Crown

10. Momentum

11. Super bowl

12. Home stretch

13. Dagger

14. Final four

15. Breakfast of champions

16. Swinging for the fences

Personalities
Page 12

1. Michael Jackson
2. Queen Latiffa
3. Babe Ruth
4. Atom Ant
5. Cher
6. Winston Churchill
7. Sting
8. Bill Gates
9. Tiger Woods
10. Lady Ga Ga
11. Flip Wilson
12. Jack Nicholson
13. Johnny Carson
14. Count Dracula
15. Christopher Columbus
16. Denzel Washington

Songs Expressions
Page 13

1. Bridge over troubled water
2. Sound of music
3. Hold on, I'm coming
4. Purple rain
5. Midnight train to Georgia
6. Bustin loose
7. Shop around
8. Reach out and touch someone's hand
9. Stop! In the name of love
10. He's got the whole world in his hands
11. I heard it through the grapevine
12.. Around the world in 80 days
i3. Poison ivy
14. Rock around the clock
15. Stormy weather
16. Tears of a clown

Songs Expressions
Page 14

1. Raindrops keep falling on my head

2. Watergate blues

3. When doves cry

4. You've lost that lovin feeling

5. My funny valentine

6. Downtown

7. No parking on the dance floor

8. Catch a falling star

9. Cloud nine

10. Mack the knife

11. Happy

12. Georgia on my mind

13. Lean on me

114. Magic carpet ride

15. What you see is what you get

16. Cry me a river

T.V. Expressions
Page 15

1. Gunsmoke
2. The Big Bang Theory
3. In the Heat of the Night
4. General Hospital
5. Duck Dynasty
6. Dancing with the stars
7. The Wire
8. Burn notice
9. Password
10. Wheel of Fortune
11. Broken arrow
12. Seinfeld
13. X Files
14. Martin
15. 20/20
16. Little House on the Prairie

T.V. Expressions
Page 16

1. Candid Camera

2. Law and Order

3. America's Most Wanted

4. Love Boat

5. Blue bloods

6. Lost

7. Mr. Ed

8. Castle

9. Judge Mathias

10. Bewitched

11. Wagon Train

12. Bones

i3. Gotham

14. Expedition Unknown

15. American Bandstand

i6. 1st (48)

Movie Expressions
Page 17

1. Iron man
2. Blazing Saddles
3. Scorpion King
4. Back to the Future
5. Batman
6. Color Purple
7. Peter Pan
8. Crouching Tiger Hidden Dragon
9. A Streetcar Named Desire
10. Pitch Back
11. Swordfish
12. The Three Hundred
i3. Love and Basketball
14. Gone in 6o Seconds
15. Tears of the Sun
i6. E.T. the Extraterrestrial

Movie Expressions
Page 18

1. The Pelican Brief

z. The Day After Tomorrow

3. Anger Management

4. Sex in the City

5. Dirty Harry

6. Dr. No

7. Friday After Next

8. Out of Africa

9. Major League

10. 101 Dalmatians

11. The Green Mile

12. Mummy

13. High Noon

14. Dances with Wolves

115. Guess Who's Coming to Dinner

16. Ghost

Potpourri
Page 19

1. The Graduate

2. Popeye

3. Not my Cup of Tea

4. Above and Beyond the Call of Duty

5. The Gift of Gab

6. Forrest Gump

7. Nat King Cole

8. Spilled Beans

9. Deer Hunter

10. Barking up the Wrong Tree

11. Mustang Sallie

12. Eraser

13. Three Part Harmony

14. Pointer Sisters

15. Ticker Tape Parade

16. A man who stands for nothing, will fall for anything

Potpourri
Page 20

1. Pirates of the Caribbean

2. Top Notch

3. Grease the Wheels

4. The pen is mightier than the sword

5. Garbage Time

6. Kojalc

7. Endless love

8. Loan shark

9. Eight mile

10. Blackball

11. Missed the boat

12. Dream Girls

13. Mask of Zorro

14. Ball Screen

15. No dice

16. No time to waste

www.ingramcontent.com/pod-product-compliance
Lightning Source LLC
Chambersburg PA
CBHW082221220526
45470CB00010B/3266